God's Promises for Your Finances

a **DOVE Christian Book** by Joseph Bartling

Do you live in bondage to your paycheck?

Sure, you believe in your old Sunday School memory verse that you cannot serve God and money...

   But ... Frankly, the paycheck pays the bills!

So you pay lip-service to putting God first.

You teach your children that the Lord will provide. And you mumble "Amen" when the pastor declares that God owns the cattle on a thousand hills and that you are heir to some of those cows. But, still, you're sure the bills won't get paid unless …

   Unless you surrender *ALL* for that all-important paycheck.

And so, you bow to the almighty dollar.

Well, it doesn't have to be that way! Are you ready for relief? Do you want to stop living in slavery? Are you tired of sacrificing your marriage, your health and your children on the golden altar of money?

God WILL provide.

Here's what you have to do.

Other fine titles from **DOVE Christian Publications:**

God's
Promises
for Your
FINANCES

by Joseph Bartling

DOVE Christian Books

Melbourne, Florida

DOVE *Christian Books*

P.O. Box 36-0122, Melbourne, FL 32936

Cover artwork by Richard Nakamoto • Editorial work and typographical design by Publications Technologies, Eau Gallie, Florida

Printed in the United States of America

DOVE Christian Books are available from good bookstores worldwide. Contact DOVE Christian Publications, 1425 Aurora Road, Melbourne, FL 32935 USA for special quantity discounts for bulk purchases for sales promotions, premiums, fund raising, evangelistic or educational use. Special books or book excerpts can also be created to fit specific needs. For details write or telephone the Marketing Department, DOVE Christian Books, 1425 Aurora Road, Melbourne, FL 32935, (407) 242-8290. **DOVE Christian Publications** are distributed in the **United States** by Spring Arbor Distribution, Ann Arbor, Michigan, as well as other fine U.S. distributors such as Whitaker House, Choice Books, Riverside, and the Zondervan Family Bookstores. In **Canada,** WORD Records, Ltd., Richmond, British Columbia. In the **United Kingdom,** Kingsway Publications, Ltd., East Sussex, England. In **Australia,** The Canterbury Press, Ltd., Scoresby, Victoria. In **New Zealand,** Omega Distributors, Ltd., Auckland. In **South Africa,** Successful Christian Living, Cape Town. In **Ghana,** Challenge Bookshops, Accra. In **Nigeria,** Lara Bookstores, Ilorin. In **Finland,** Cross-Curtain Communications, Helsinki. In **Singapore,** Christian Growth Bookstores, Singapore. In **South America,** Principios de Vida, Bacacay 3706, 5009 Córdoba, Republica Argentina

DEDICATION

To my loving "helpmeet," Karen, who by the Spirit encourages me to practice what I preach.

TABLE OF CONTENTS

God's Promises for Your Finances

INTRODUCTION

"... but lay up for yourselves treasures in heaven, where neither moth or rust destroys and where thieves do not break in or steal" (Matthew 6:20).

Biblical financial principles are so tragically ignored today! Fine Christian families live in bondage to their paychecks! We know in our hearts that we cannot serve God and money — but we are caught in Satan's trap anyway!

So we pay lip-service to the idea of putting God first, teach that truth to our children and mumble "Amen" when the pastor declares it from the pulpit...

But, still, the hard cold fact is that *money* pays the bills.

So, ashamed that we cannot live what we believe, we self-righteously proclaim "to God be the glory," then privately do *whatever* we have to do scrape together the meager cash needed to provide our wants and desires.

That's slavery!

And it's **unnecessary,** friends!

Christians are bound up in "hand-to-mouth" existences — living paycheck-to-paycheck. They are crippled with awesome interest payments on credit-card and home-mortgage debt. Their hearts are filled with guilt over having to work two and three jobs. Their marriages, children and spiritual lives are neglected as they toil away, laying their sacrifices on the golden altar of money.

How many times have you seen Satan buy out a Christian? The devout mother is determined to stay home and nurture her pre-schoolers in the way of the Lord. But the family really needs a mini-van. So, she takes on a 25-hour-a-week job that turns into 45 hours a week. She grows more and more frazzled. The pre-schoolers grow more and more pagan, unruly and emotionally stunted as they are raised by strangers.

And what about the Christian man who abandons ethical principles when it will cost him money to stick to his righteousness?

What a disaster!

Blindly, he is giving up incredible prosperity! God gives us a way to live in his provision *and it works!* Satan's traps of greed, covetousness and materialism do *not!*

Jesus spent many hours teaching financial principles to His disciples, and one thing was clear: With a thorough understanding of God's financial principles, we can understand how God's kingdom operates in the realm of the Spirit as well. Jesus said this in Mark 4:11-14:

> *"To you has been given the mystery of the kingdom of God...Do you not understand this parable? And how will you understand all the parables?"*

I want to teach you what the Bible teaches about money and how you can practically apply God's kingdom principles to your daily life. It doesn't matter whether you are a multi-millionaire or unemployed or thousands of dollars in debt. God's principles work the same for everyone when they are applied.

Even if you are not a Christian, this book will give you valuable keys that, if followed, will prosper you to some degree. Throughout history, God's Jewish people have benefited from God's financial laws — evidence that applying His laws works.

"True" prosperity is not measured with "dollars in the bank." It is God's will that you "prosper and be in health, just as your soul prospers" (3 John 2). In this book, you will learn about tithing and how, through the tithe, God can establish His covenant with you individually. You will learn practical ways of getting out of debt and staying that way. You will also learn how to trust God for large items, like cars and houses, without borrowing.

No, I'm not saying that you can "name it and claim it." We're not going to go lay hands on a Mercedes-Benz and declare it ours in Jesus' name. But we are going to learn how to trust the Lord. If you can't trust God for a parking place at your job, you certainly are not going to be able to trust Him for a paid-for house. But as your faith grows, you will find it exciting to walk and live by faith. You will give God more and more opportunities to be God in your life.

You will learn how to control your monthly cash flow through God's plan of stewardship, telling your money where to go, instead of wondering where it went. You will learn a basic investment strategy to maximize returns for God's glory, and how to live abundantly through giving. Lastly, we will discuss how to use your prosperity for the glory of God.

I pray, in Jesus' name, that you will prayerfully read each chapter in this book in order, with your Bible and your heart open to receive God's Word to you. Faith comes by hearing and hearing by the word of God (Romans 10:17). Your faith will grow, and grow, and grow as you receive the word. Act upon it and God will make every promise in His word come alive in your life.

1. "TRUE" PROSPERITY: FIRST THINGS FIRST

"...I came that they might have life and have it more abundantly. "John 10:10

"TRUE" PROSPERITY: FIRST THINGS FIRST

My desktop dictionary gives this definition for the word "abundant":

Present in great quantity; abounding; richly supplied; having an abundance of good things.

Many of us have tried to live an abundant life without a personal relationship with the living God through Jesus Christ.

We've all heard of millionaires living in fear and misery every day of their lives. The spiritual danger of this type of life manifests itself in ulcers, heart disease, high blood pressure and other ailments. In a constant atmosphere of anxiety, few people with material wealth can enjoy "true" prosperity. I can declare this boldly because James 1:17 says,

"Every good thing and every perfect gift is from above, coming down from the Father of lights."

The only way to enjoy "true" prosperity, fulfillment, and contentment in your life is to be able to tap into the riches of God. His riches include peace, joy, love, patience, freedom and victory, in addition to gold, silver, and cattle on a thousand hills.

You can, through a personal relationship with Jesus Christ, enjoy that fulfillment of abundant life in its ultimate fullness, an eternal life with no fear of death. Romans 10:12,13 says,

"For there is no distinction between Jew and Greek; for the same Lord is Lord of all abounding in riches for all who call upon Him; for whosoever shall call upon the name of the Lord will be saved."

Jesus Christ was given to the world, because of God's love for us, to die for you so that you can have an abundant, victorious, eternal life (John 3:16). It takes the life of God Almighty imparted to you to give you life. Many Christians call this being "born-again" or "born from above." That's what Jesus called it too! In John 3:3, Jesus says to the religious man, Nicodemus, and to you also,

"Unless a man is born again, he cannot see the kingdom of God."

When you receive Jesus as your personal Savior, God gives you the power to become a son of God (John 1:12).

You can know God through Jesus Christ and become born-again right where you are, by confessing with your mouth Jesus as Lord of your life, and believing with your heart that God raised Him from the dead. For with the heart man believes resulting in righteousness, and with the mouth he confesses, resulting in salvation. (Romans 10:9,10)

If you have not received Jesus Christ as your Savior and Lord, please take a minute, set this book down, and ask Jesus into your life. I'll wait until you are done praying...

Now that you are back, let's go on with our teaching. Oh, by the way, welcome into the kingdom of God if you have just now asked Jesus into your life. As you prayed that prayer of salvation to God, you became my brother or sister in the Lord Jesus, and are destined for an eternal home in heaven with God! *Hallelujah!*

I wish I could talk with you in person, but since that's not possible, I'd like you to find a pastor to talk to about your new faith. If you don't know a clergyman, get out your Yellow Pages and looking under "Churches" find the "Non-Denominational" column. Now, pick out a church that uses words such as "faith," "joy" and "Bible" in its Yellow Pages ad. If there aren't any, steer clear of the Mormons, Unitarians, Jehovah's Witnesses and Christian Scientists and look for a church whose ad indicates that they believe the Bible.

Call up the pastor! Why? Because the Bible tells us not to try to serve the Lord all by ourselves. We're supposed to fellowship by worshiping and praying with other Christians. Introduce yourself to the pastor, tell him what you've just done and ask when you can come by and meet him — and talk about what else you need to do as a new Christian.

Now, back to the topic at hand.

Finances — and God's promises! In Colossians 3:3 we find that "our life is hidden with Christ in God." The riches of Christ are "unfathomable" (Ephesians 3:8). I guess that means that we shouldn't even try to fathom them. But this I know, "true" prosperity is living in the Spirit of God, letting the peace of Christ rule in your hearts, to which we were called in one body. Letting the word of Christ richly dwell within you, with all wisdom, teaching and understanding, and admonishing one another with psalms and hymns and spiritual songs, singing with thankfulness in our hearts to God. (Colossians 3:15-17)

"True" prosperity is allowing God to be God in your life. We must do that so that He can accomplish His plan through us on this earth. When we sacrifice our own life completely to Him, we must present our bodies, a living and holy sacrifice, acceptable to God, which is our spiritual service of worship (Romans 12:1).

"True" prosperity is the result of a life that is totally submitted, committed, consecrated and dedicated to God. Jesus said,

> *"Truly I say to you, there is no one who has left house or brothers or sisters or mother or father or children or farms, for My sake and for the Gospel's sake, but that he shall receive a hundred times as much* **now in this present age,** *houses, and brothers and sisters and mothers and children and farms, along with persecutions; and in the age to come, eternal life" (Mark 10:29,30).*

Jesus has promised to give us a hundredfold returnif we give for His sake and the Gospel's sake.

A word of warning: You cannot please God by loving Him more than you love money! *You cannot love money at all!* The Bible says,

> *"No man can serve two masters; for either he will hate the one and love the other, or he will hold to one and despise the other. You cannot serve God and mammon (wealth)" (Matthew 6:24).*

I've had brothers in the Lord come to me and have told me that they have had to make a decision to either pay their tithe or pay their bills. Many must choose between tithing to God and a new car or a new house. According to the Bible, there is no choice! You cannot serve God and riches! During this Sermon on the Mount, Jesus didn't even preach on about serving riches. He knew that for the true believer, its just plain as day, You will serve God and God only (Exodus 20:5)!.

The rich young ruler lacked only one thing to become "truly" prosperous. He had material wealth, the Bible says that he was rich. Let's look at the story.

> *"And when He (Jesus) was setting out on a journey, a man ran up to Him and knelt before Him, and began asking Him, 'Good teacher, what shall I do to inherit eternal life?'" (It is interesting to note that he was not satisfied even though he was rich.)*
>
> *And Jesus said to him, 'Why do you call me good? No one is good except God alone. You know the commandments, 'Do not murder, do not commit*

adultery, do not steal, do not bear false witness, do not defraud, honor thy father and mother.' And he said to Him, 'Teacher, I have kept all these things from my youth up.'

And looking at him, Jesus felt a love for him, and said to him, One thing you lack: Go and sell all you possess, and give to the poor, and you shall have treasure in heaven, and come follow Me.' (Mark 10:17-21)

Now, I've heard people preach that the "one thing" the man lacked was that he "had" a lot of possessions. But its obvious that that is not a "lack" at all. What did the man lack? He lacked a giving heart. Jesus told this man to "go and GIVE." He was in bondage to his possessions. He could not give them, because he loved them. To him, his possessions were his life. He was motivated out of greed, not out of love. Jesus said, "Beware, and be on your guard against EVERY form of greed; for not even when one has an abundance (This must be OK with Jesus), does his life consist of his possessions (Luke 12:15).

"True" prosperity is not "things." "True" prosperity is "life," the abundant life! In the Greek it is "Zoe" — "absolute" life.

Now that we understand what "true" prosperity is, we can discuss God's plan for your finances, knowing that God wants you to be "truly" prosperous, even as your soul prospers...

2. GOD'S PLAN FOR YOUR PROSPERITY

"But you shall remember the Lord your God, for it is He who is giving you the power to make wealth, that He may establish His covenant which He swore to your fathers, as it is this day."
Deuteronomy 8:18

GOD'S PLAN FOR YOUR PROSPERITY

God wants you to be prosperous! Many of us have been under religious teaching that tells us that God wants us poor.

The Bible tells us that we must not invalidate the Word of God with our traditions (Matthew 16:5). We as the Body of Christ must recognize God's financial plan for us , and line our minds and attitudes up to what the Word of God says, and not what our tradition or previous teaching might be. God's financial plan is evident from the above scripture.

First, we must remember the Lord our God.

Remembering God must be the first priority in any believer's life. Matthew 6:33

says, "Seek first the kingdom of God and His righteousness, and all these things will be added unto you."

Secondly, remember the source of wealth:

Deuteronomy 8:18 shows us that God gives us the power to make wealth, so making wealth cannot in itself be evil.

"But you shall remember the Lord your God, for it is He who is giving you the power to make wealth, that He may establish His covenant which He swore to your fathers, as it is this day." (Deuteronomy 8:18).

All increase is of the Lord. Mark 4:26-28 says,

"The kingdom of God is like a man who casts seed upon the soil; and goes to bed at night and gets up by day, and the seed sprouts up and grows, how he himself does not know. The soil produces crops of itself, first the blade, then the head, then the mature grain in the head."

All of God's creation is governed by law, principles that He ordained. These include physical laws like gravity and thermodynamics. There are also many principles in the Spirit realm. Romans 8:2 says,

> *"For the law of the Spirit of life in Christ Jesus has set you free from the law of sin and death."*

So the life in Christ Jesus is governed by the law of the Spirit, or by spiritual law. The law described in Mark 4:26-28 is the Law of Increase. I Corinthians 3:7 says,

> *"So then neither the one who plants nor the one who waters is anything, but God who causes the growth."*

Our God is a God of life and reproduction. It is clear that God wants His Word multiplied in the earth" (Acts 12:24).

God's plan is to cause growth in ALL areas of His kingdom, whether it is in souls, the Word of God, crops, or in the prosperity of His covenant people.

Thirdly, God wants to bless us.

He wants to establish His covenant in our lives. He does this by giving us the power to make wealth, and blessing whatever we do. Deuteronomy 28:1 says,

"Now it shall be, if you diligently obey the Lord your God, being careful to do all His commandments which I command you today, the Lord your God will set you high above all the nations of the earth."

Now that's establishing a covenant! He goes on to say,

"And all these blessings shall come upon you and overtake you, if you will obey the Lord your God. Blessed shall you be in the city, blessed shall you be in the country, blessed shall be the off-spring of your body and the produce of your ground and the offspring of your beasts, the increase of your herd and the young of your flock. Blessed shall be your basket and your kneading bowl. Blessed shall you be when you come in, and blessed shall you be when you go out. The Lord will cause your enemies who rise up against you to be defeated before you; they shall come out against you one way and shall flee be-

fore you seven ways. The **Lord will command the blessing upon you in your barns and in all you put your hand to,** and He will bless you in the land which the Lord your God gives you.

The Lord **will establish you** as a holy people to Himself, as He swore to you, **if** you will keep the commandment of the Lord your God and **walk** in His ways.

So all the peoples of the earth shall see **that you are called by the name of the Lord;** and they shall be afraid of you. And the Lord will **make you abound in prosperity,** in the offspring of your body and in the offspring of your beasts and in the produce of your ground, in the land which the Lord swore to your fathers to give you.

The Lord will open for you His good storehouse, the heavens, to give rain to your land in its season and to bless **all the work of your hand;** and you shall lend to many, **but you shall not borrow.**

And the Lord shall make you the head and not the tail, and you only shall be above, and you shall not be underneath, if you will listen to the commandments of the Lord your God, which I charge you today, to observe them carefully." (Deuteronomy 28:2-13)

Fourthly, we are heirs!

The Lord has sworn this to our fathers. Galatians 3:29 says,

> "If you belong to Christ, then you are Abraham's seed, and heirs according to the promise."

Romans 9:6-8 says,

> "For they are **not** all Israel who are descended from Israel; neither are they all children because they are Abraham's descendants, but "through Isaac your descendants will be named."

It is not the children of the flesh who are children of God, but the children of promise are regarded as descendants. Galatians 3:16 says,

> "Now the promises were spoken to Abraham and to his seed, He does not

*say 'and to seeds' as referring to many, but rather to one, and to your **seed which is Christ.***"

And according to Galatians 3:29, we have as much right to the blessing of Abraham as Christ did, because we are in Christ and as such,**we are the seed of Abraham,** and heirs according to the promise. Hallelujah!

Genesis 17:7 says,

"And I will establish My covenant between Me and you (Abraham) and your seed (that's us — Gal. 3:29) after you throughout their generations for an everlasting covenant, to be God to you and to your seed (us) after you.

I've heard from religious teachers that God wants us to have "spiritual" prosperity, not "financial" prosperity. The Bible says,

*"The Lord your God is bringing you into a good land, a land of brooks of water, of fountains and springs, flowing forth in valleys and hills; a land of wheat and barley, of vines and fig trees and pomegranates, a land of olive oil and honey; a land where you shall eat food **without scarcity,** in which you will not lack **anything;** a land whose*

*stones are iron, and out of hills you can dig copper. When you have eaten and are satisfied, you shall bless the Lord your God for the good land which He has given you. Beware lest you forget the Lord your God by not keeping His commandments and His ordinances and His statutes which I am commanding today; lest when you have eaten and are satisfied, and have built houses and lived in them, and when your herds and your flocks multiply, and **your silver and gold multiplies.** (Deuteronomy 8:7-13)*

If we keep God's commandments and walk in His word and obey the voice of God, He will bless us in all that we do. That's what the Bible says, so I believe it! Walking in this manner will produce blessings from God. God even warns us to remember Him first so as not to be proud and trust in the riches. The story of the rich young ruler in the New Testament bears witness that keeping these commandments will cause the blessings to come upon us. In Mark 10, Jesus is explaining the kingdom of God to the rich young ruler. Jesus tells him, "If you wish to enter into life, keep the commandments."

The ruler said, "Teacher, I have kept all these things from my youth up" (v. 20). Jesus said, "One thing you lack; go and sell all you possess, and give to the poor, and you shall have treasure in heaven; and come, follow Me." (v. 21) "But at these words, his face fell, and he went away grieved, for he was one who owned much property." (Mark 10:22)

This man had kept the covenant and all its statutes, and God had established His covenant with him. But the man broke the covenant when he forgot the Lord and let his heart get proud, just as God had warned in Deuteronomy 8:11. It was not wrong for the man to have wealth, in fact, God had caused the wealth to come upon him. This man had been walking in the covenant. His problem was that his heart had turned from God and was set on the riches. his problem was the "love of money," not the money itself.

Surely we can expect the blessing of God to come upon us as we walk in covenant with Him. We must always keep God first, and if we don't, God will not allow us to keep it. The Bible says that "prosperity will ruin a fool" (Proverbs 1:32).

Fifthly, the Lord does not change.

God's covenant is "as it is this day." In fact, if Jesus appeared to you today and promised it to you in your living room, His covenant with you wouldn't be any firmer than the covenant that He has already made to you through your father in faith, Abraham. Your covenant (as the "seed" of Abraham) and Abraham's covenant are identical, in fact, its the same covenant. Not only will His covenant be established in heaven, but it will be established on earth too! Jesus, in teaching the disciples to pray, prayed that "Thy kingdom come, thy will be done, on earth as it is in heaven" (Matthew 5:10). God's covenant is already established in heaven. Jesus established it when He entered the Holy of Holies in heaven with His own blood, once and for all having obtained eternal redemption (Hebrews 9:12).

God surrounds himself with the beauty of his creation. The city of God is pure gold, like clear glass, and the foundation stones of the city wall are adorned with every kind of precious stone (Revelation 21:18,19). We are his children, and joint-heirs with Jesus. He desires us to abound in the beauty of His creation. Haggai 2:9 says,

"The glory of the latter house is greater than the glory of the former."

We, the Church of Jesus Christ, are the latter house (I Peter 2:5),

And none of us have exceeded Solomon's glory yet. It will be done, says the Lord. We have a better covenant than they did, founded on more precious promises (Heb. 8:6).

Our God is a *today* God. He is the great "I AM." No future, no past. Everything in God's kingdom is "today." "Today" is the day of salvation. "Today" if you hear his voice, harden not your heart. Jesus is the same yesterday, today, and forever (Hebrews 13:8). He is always in the "now." He wants to establish His covenant "now." in the earth. He wants you to prosper, now. He wants to set you up on high above the nations, now. He wants to set you free from financial bondage, now!

3. GOD'S YARDSTICK FOR YOUR PROSPERITY

"This book of the law shall not depart from thy mouth, but you shall meditate on it day and night, so that you may be careful to do all that is written in it; for then you will make your way prosperous, and then you will have success." Joshua 1:8

GOD'S YARDSTICK FOR YOUR PROSPERITY

We all know that God is no respecter of persons. But many of us have disregarded what the Bible says simply because we've watched someone live a godly life — someone who had it rough financially his entire life or didn't get healed every time he prayed.

I don't completely understand why some believers can apply God's word and others can't, but I do know this:

God's word is true.

It's not God's fault if someone has not applied His principles. Notice how many times the word "you" or "thy" is used in the above scripture. God has placed the burden upon *US* to choose to abide in His word. We must not only "meditate," but also to "do all." The

45

only way to accomplish this in our life is by faith.

True, God is not a respecter of persons, but He is a respecter of faith. This is obvious when reading the eleventh chapter of the book of Hebrews, the "Hall of Faith."

> *"Without faith it is impossible to please Him, for he who comes to God must believe that He is, and that He is a rewarder of those who diligently seek Him" (Hebrews 11:6).*

There He goes again with "our part," diligently seeking him.

God's yardstick for prospering you is determined by the prosperity of your soul. 3 John 2 says,

> *"I pray that you may prosper and be in health, as your soul prospers."*

Remember that this is not the recreated spirit, the new creature in Christ Jesus. We are a spirit, we have a soul, and we live in a body. Our soul consists of our will, our intellect, and our emotions. These are not recreated in the new birth. Our minds must be "renewed" by the word of God (Romans 12:2).

We are to "take every thought captive to the obedience of Christ" (2 Cor. 10:5). We must "put on the new man" (Eph. 4:24). James 1:21 says we are to "put aside all filthiness and all that remains of wickedness, in humility receive the engrafted word, which is able to save our soul (will, intellect, and emotions)."

Let me emphasize, though, that we, in our own fleshly strength, cannot accomplish this. It can be accomplished only through our abiding in the word of God. In effect, the Bible tells us that your financial prosperity and your good health is in direct proportion to the prosperity of your soul, which is the "storehouse" of the engrafted word. Many well-meaning Christians believe that God brings them along in faith and it is his decision to prosper some and not prosper others. Actually, God can only bring to pass in this earth what we allow Him to bring to pass.

> *"Truly whatever we bind on earth is bound in heaven, and whatever we loose on earth is loosed in heaven"* *(Matt. 16:19).*

He has given the human race dominion on this planet, just as He gave to Adam in the book of Genesis, and will not contradict the integrity of His word. Many times we bind God from establishing His covenant in the earth through our unbelief. Jesus was bound from performing miracles and healings in Nazareth because of their unbelief (Mark 6:5,6). It must have been God's will and desire to heal them because Psalm 103:3 says,

> *"He heals all of our diseases"*

Exodus 15:26 says,

> *"I am the God that healeth thee."*

God's character does not change (Psalms 15:4). If unbelief could stop the Son of God from performing miracles then, even when He wanted to, then certainly unbelief stops God today in the same way. I wonder how much Jesus marvels at the unbelief in the Church today! Our father in faith, Abraham,

> *"staggered not at the promise of God through unbelief, but was strong in faith, giving glory to God, and being fully persuaded that what He*

promised, He was able to perform, and therefore (or as a result of His faith) it was imputed to him for righteousness (Romans 4:20-22).

Do you stagger at the promises of God's covenant to you, His covenant child? Or are you strong in faith, giving glory to God and fully persuaded that what God promised in His word to you, He is able and wills to perform it in your life? James 1:6,7 says,

"Let Him ask in faith without any doubting, for the one who doubts is like the surf of the sea driven and tossed by the wind. For let not that man expect that he will receive anything from the Lord."

Thank God that He has given us the mystery of the kingdom of God (Mark 4:11)! We know that

"Faith cometh by hearing and hearing by the word of God" (Romans 10:17).

So in order to build up our faith to receive what God has promised in His word, we must commit ourselves 100 percent to the word of God. We must believe and act upon every single word. We must surround ourselves completely with HIS word.

God, in giving instruction to Joshua on how to possess the land given to the sons of Israel said,

> *"This book of the law shall not depart from your mouth, but you shall meditate on it day and night, so that you may be careful to do all that is written in it, for then you will make your way prosperous and then you will have success" (Joshua 1:8).*

Jesus said,

> *"If any man have ears to hear, let him hear. Take care what you listen to. By your standard of measure, it shall be measured to you, and to you who hear, more shall be given." (Mark 4:23,24)*

Jesus had just explained how the kingdom of God works, the 30-, 60- and 100-fold return. He's just told us that the measure that we measure with (or hear the Word of God), whether 30-, 60- or 100-fold, will be the measure that God uses to measure back to us. He has made the 100-fold return available to everyone that will hear, but only the ones who measure their hearing with a 100-fold measure will receive the 100-fold return.

Satan attempts to bombard us with things "in our ears." He knows the principles of God too! If he can choke the word of God going into your ears with TV, radio, movies, newspapers, football games and the like, he knows that the measure of the word of God entering your ears has been thwarted to some degree. He knows that when the word of God enters your ears, and then your heart, there will be growth (Mark 4:26-28). Plain arithmetic will prove to you, that if you hear the word of God for 1 hour a week, and hear 40 hours of secular TV (even news broadcasts), your return cannot be 100-fold.

We have a choice to hear the word of God or not. But once we've made the choice, the effects of the words entering into our soul will have their effect. Pastor Peter Lord says that words entering your soul are like food entering into your stomach. You have the choice whether to eat a banana, or a piece of candy. Once you've made a choice and started eating the candy, you cannot stop the effects of the candy once ingested by your body. Your body will "count" every calorie (whether you count them or not!) and the sugar will penetrate into your system. But if you've chosen the banana, the nutrients in that banana will also nourish your body, and the vitamins will penetrate your body as well.

You can choose to surround yourself with the word of God. Listen to tapes proclaiming the glorious Gospel of Jesus Christ. I've spent entire weekends listening to nothing but teaching tapes. Get a New Testament on tape and listen to it regularly. Just one hour of driving per day can be redeemed by listening to God's word. You'd be surprised how many hours per week you can choose to absorb God's word into your ears and heart, and you'll be healthier and happier for it.

Proverbs 4:20-23 says,

"My son, give attention to my words; incline your ear to my sayings. Do not let them depart from your sight; Keep then in the midst of your heart. For they (the words) are life to those who find them, and health to all their

whole body. watch over your heart with all diligence, for from it flow the springs of life."

Once the word of God is in your heart, you must act on it. You must believe that God wants you to be obedient, diligent in keeping the commandments and you must walk in them. James 2:17 says,

"Faith, without works (corresponding action), is dead, being by itself."

If you really believe something in your heart, you will act on it.

*"Prove yourselves **doers** of the word, and not merely hearers only"* *(James 1:22).*

You must do the word of God. When it says give, you must give. When it says tithe, you must tithe. When it says forgive, you must forgive. When it says repent, you must repent. Obedience is the key to receiving from God.

Jesus says in Matthew 7:24-27,

*"Therefore everyone who **hears** these words of Mine, and **acts upon them,** may be compared to a **wise***

*man, who built his house upon a rock.
And the rain descended, and the floods
came, and the winds blew, and burst
against the house; and yet it did not
fall, for it had been founded upon the
rock. And everyone who **hears** these
words of **mine,** and **does not act** upon
them, will be like a **foolish** man, who
built his house upon the sand. And the
rain descended, and the floods came,
and the winds blew, and burst against
that house, and it fell, and great was
its fall."*

"Hearing these words" was not enough.
You can believe that every word of the Bible
from Genesis to Revelation *is* the word of
God, but if you do not act upon it, you are
believing only from your head. You may have
believed that "If you confess with your
mouth Jesus is Lord, and believe in your
heart that God raised Him from the dead,
you shall be saved."

Just believing that you ought to confess
Jesus is Lord will not result in your salvation. Only by *confessing* with your mouth
(acting on the word) will result in your salvation (Romans 10:9,10). You will confess

only if you truly believe from your heart (not your head).

You must act as if every word in the Bible is true (because it is!). The Bible says,

> *"You are the righteousness of God in Christ Jesus" (II Cor. 5:21).*

It doesn't matter if you just committed a sin one minute ago. The Bible still says that I am the righteousness of God in Christ Jesus, and I believe it. Glory to God! I am made righteous by my faith in Him, and what He has done for me, by dying on the cross and shedding His blood, not in the fact that I just sinned or not.

If the Bible says that "God heals all my diseases" (Psalms 103:3), then God heals all my diseases. If the Bible says God will establish His covenant between Him and the "seed" of Abraham to multiply him exceedingly, then Praise the Lord, that means me! I am the "seed" of Abraham; that's what the Bible says, (Gal. 3:29).

We must *act* like Abraham, and call into being that which does not exist in the physical world (Romans 4:17) to cause to come to pass in the physical world, that which already exists in the spiritual world. (Charles Capps has an excellent tape series on this subject called *Calling Things That Are Not*).

"For we look not at the things which are seen, but at the things that are not seen; for the things which are seen are temporal, but the things which are not seen are eternal" (II Cor. 4:18).

Acting on the word takes faith, but it also brings great rewards, and pleases God (Hebrews 11:6). It takes His faith. It is His command in Mark 11:22, "Have the faith of God." Remember, the yardstick for God establishing His covenant with you is the yardstick you use in measuring His word into your heart and the measure that you act upon it!

4. GOD'S REASON FOR PROSPERING YOU

"If you then, being evil, know how to give good gifts to your children, how much more shall your Father who is in heaven give what is good to those who ask Him." Matthew 7:11

GOD'S REASON FOR PROSPERING YOU

God has said in His Word that He wants us to prosper and be in health, even as our soul prospers (3 John 2). Matthew 7:11 tells us that it gives God pleasure to give us good things, just as we, as earthly fathers, like to give good things to our children. But God does not give us "things" just so we can cart them around and hoard them for some "rainy day." Of course, He gives us "things" because He loves us, and He wants us to have them. But God's reason for prospering His people goes much deeper than that.

His primary reason for prospering you is so that, through you, the Gospel can be preached to every creature. (Mark 16:15) Have you ever figured out how much it would cost to "go into all the world"? Kenneth Copeland said recently that it will take a billion dollars to win the continent of Africa to Jesus Christ. As long as the Body of Christ's money is "tied up" in other things (like debt), the Gospel cannot be preached to every creature. Friends, Jesus can not come back until the Gospel is preached to every creature. Jesus Himself said in Matthew 24:14,

> *"And this gospel of the kingdom shall be preached in all the world for a witness unto all nations; and then shall the end come."*

I believe that many believers will have to answer to God for the unfaithful way that they have handled the blessings of God. Right now, in Africa, there is one person saved for every $3 invested in missions there. Now that's some heavenly treasure!

In these last days, God is mightily using television and satellite technology to bring the world the message of the kingdom. I prophesy that one of the major U.S. television networks will be bought out by a syndicate of Christian businessmen within the next ten years. Christian businessmen all over America will be led of the Spirit of God to buy out secular TV and radio stations, and they will be extremely prosperous.

Do you realize that if every Christian family in America would commit a $100 gift to Christian radio and TV, the exposure of the gospel would reach out to every community. If the world is watching TV, then we're going to have to preach the gospel to them on TV! We need to meet the people right where they are. In Jesus' day, if the people were in the synagogue, that's where Jesus went to preach to them. If they were at the house of publicans, that's where Jesus went to preach to them. (Note that the disciples "followed" Jesus into Levi's house. I think we should "follow" Jesus into the world's houses.)

I know that the Bible says,

> *"Come out and be ye separate saith the Lord" (II Cor. 6:17).*

Let me ask you a question: Did Jesus sit and eat with the sinners or not? (Mark 2:15 has the answer.) Another question: Was Jesus separated from sinners? The Bible says about Jesus,

"...seeing He ever liveth to make intercession for them. For such a high priest became us, who is holy, harmless, and undefiled, separate from sinners, and made higher than the heavens. (Hebrews 7:25,26)

We stay "separated from sinners" by not "yoking" with them. (The grammar may not be correct, but it gets the point across!)

We need to go into every highway, byway, country, island and sea and literally blanket this earth with the gospel. It will take a lot of money. It may take a trillion dollars, but I'm not worried. That's just a drop in the bucket for my Heavenly Father. He is my "El Shaddai," the God who is more than enough! If it takes $100 trillion, He'll provide $200 trillion! And I've got news for you: Every dollar of that will come from the hands of born-again believers who will trust God to make the most out of every "seed." It will be given in faith, or it will not be used of the Lord.

You see, it is impossible to blanket this earth with the gospel of Jesus unless it comes through the hands of God's people, the

Body of Christ. If every one of us took a vow of poverty, we couldn't scrape up enough money to buy a tract, much less a Bible. Even Jesus' ministry required money. His ministry needed so much money to meet the needs of the people, that they had a full-time treasurer to handle the finances. And how do you think "the seventy" were supported when they went "full-time." Can you imagine how much Zaccheus gave to the ministry of Jesus. He said that he was giving half of what he owned to the poor, and the Bible says that he was "very rich." (Luke 19:2)

Jesus succeeded in giving away everything he owned before He died. II Corinthians 8:9 says,

> *"For ye know the grace of our Lord Jesus Christ, that, though He was rich, yet for your sakes he became poor, that ye (that means me and you too!), through His poverty, might be rich."*

Jesus gave everything away as an example for us. He didn't "grasp" the things of this world. He knew what He had to do to reconcile the world to Himself. He did His part. It's up to us to do our part. By and through the leading of the Spirit of God, we must finance this last-days explosion of evangelism all over the world as never before, so that Jesus can come back all the sooner!

5. THE TITHE — A HOLY THING TO GOD

"All the tithe of the land, of the seed of the land or of the fruit of the tree, is the Lord's; it is holy to the Lord."
Leviticus 27:30

THE TITHE — A HOLY THING TO GOD

Operating under God's economic system requires some knowledge of how it operates. Most believers know that they "should" tithe at least 10 percent of their income to the Lord, but many don't know why or how the tithe operates.

The first step in getting your finances aligned with God's economic system is to tithe. It doesn't matter how much in debt you are, or how wealthy you are. It doesn't matter how many months you may be behind in your bills.

You must start tithing immediately. The reason for this is very clear from Malachi 3:8,9, "Will a man rob God? Yet you are robbing Me! But you say, 'How have we robbed Thee?,' In tithes and offerings. You are cursed with a curse, for you are robbing Me, the whole nation of you!" These were God's chosen people, the people of God, just as we are in the New Covenant.

You cannot get out from under the effects of a curse unless you first are freed from the curse itself. The effects of the curse are described in Mal. 3:11,

"the devourer destroys the fruits of the ground and your vine casts its self."

Have you ever felt like someone was taking every dollar out of your checkbook before you even see it? The curse is in operation! You get out from under the curse by applying the solution outlined in Malachi 3:10,

'Bring the whole tithe into the storehouse, so that there may be food in My house, and test me now in this' says the Lord of hosts, 'if I will not open for you the windows of heaven, and pour out for you a blessing until it overflows.'

My first experience with scriptural tithing came at a point in my financial life that I truly needed a miracle. I had just closed a retail store and had an immediate (within 30 days) cash need of over $25,000. I needed a "window-full" to get me out. After reading Malachi 3:8-11, I realized that the reason I was in financial bondage was that the curse was operating in full force in my life.

The devourer was eating every dime that had been coming in to the business. If the curse could be working with that much effectiveness, I knew that the blessing could also work with the same effectiveness, but in the positive direction In the worst financial condition of my entire life, *I STARTED TITHING.*

I stepped out in faith to believe God that His word was true and that the blessings would flow. In fact, I had to trust Him for a full one hundred-fold return. I needed it, and I needed it fast. I remember the words I used: "Lord, this tithe represents my giving of my first-fruits to you. You said in your Word to prove you NOW in this, so here I go. I'm trusting you NOW Lord, for a full hundred-fold return on this tithe, in Jesus' name. The next day I received a check from an unexpected source for $185.

And that was just the start. Checks started coming in from all over. It worked so well that first week, that I decided to tithe twice as much the next week. That week, checks for hundreds of dollars started coming in from all over the nation. Property and inventory that I had been trying to sell for months started selling, and at good prices too. I kept on tithing, and God kept on showering overflowing blessings.

Four days before the $25,000 cash was due, I had commitments that the amount would be paid and the matter settled. As I walked out of the office, free of the $25,000 debt, my eyes were directed to a Bible on the table in the corner of the waiting room. The Lord spoke to me in my spirit saying clearly, "I will meet all you needs according to My riches in glory if you will let Me be God in your finances." Praise the Lord for miracles! He truly does meet our needs, and just in time!

The Lord began to show me why tithing the tithe was so critical to His economic plan. We all know that "the earth is the Lord's and the fullness thereof" (Ps. 24:1). Psalms 2:8 says of Jesus, that

> *"He has been given the nations and the very ends of the earth as His possession."*

So Jesus legally owns the earth and everything in it! Now look at this: Leviticus 27:30 says,

> *"All the tithe of the land, of the seed of the land, or of the fruit of the tree, is the Lord's; it is HOLY to the Lord."*

Wilson's *Old Testament Word Studies* defines "holy" as "something sacred, consecrated to God, free from defilement, of vice, idolatry, and other impure and profane things."

In the light of Leviticus 27:30, tithing began in the garden of Eden, even before Adam's fall. The Lord God commanded that Adam could eat of any trees in the garden except one, the tree of the knowledge of good and evil. That tree was the "tithe of the land," the tithe of the garden of Eden. As soon as Adam and Eve, "robbed" from that tithe by eating of its fruit, the curse of eternal separation from God was upon them.

Abel brought his "tithe," the firstlings of his flock, and the fat thereof. He brought that which was "holy," consecrated and set apart for God (see Lev. 3:16,17). Cain only brought "an offering." He didn't give God his first-fruits. There was nothing wrong with the substance. Cain was a tiller of the ground, and as such, didn't have a lamb for his offering. Deuteronomy 26 says that the first-fruits of the ground are acceptable, but nowhere does it imply that Cain brought his first-fruits. I understand that "without the shedding of blood there is no remission of sin," but this sacrifice was not for sin. It was not for their redemption. God had not given them a plan of redemption. Cain's problem was that He rebelled against God by bringing what HE wanted to bring, instead of bringing his first-fruits. Cain was cursed in Genesis 4:11, not just because he killed his brother, but because he "robbed" the holy tithe from the Lord. And read this:

*"When Joshua was leading the sons of Israel into the land to possess it, he was standing near Jericho. He was met by a man standing with his sword drawn in his hand. The man said, "I indeed come now as the captain of the host of the Lord'. And Joshua fell on his face to the earth and bowed down, and said to him, 'What has my lord to say to his servant?,' And the captain of the Lord's host said to Joshua, 'Remove your sandals from your feet, for the place where you are standing is **HOLY,'** and Joshua did so." (Joshua 5:13-15)*

Jericho was holy, but Ai was not. No angel or man appeared to Joshua at Ai, and he didn't have to take off his shoes! The reason that Jericho was holy was because it was the first city, the "first-fruits" of the land that had been given them to possess, and as such was "holy" as a tithe unto the Lord.

"Joshua said to the people, "Shout! For the Lord has given you the city. And the city shall be under the ban (or curse, Heb. cherum — a devoted thing; that which is separated or appointed to destruction.) it and all that is in it belongs to the Lord...But as for you, only `

*keep yourselves from the things under the ban, lest you covet them and take some of the things under the ban, so you would make the camp of Israel **ACCURSED** and bring trouble on it. But all the silver and gold and articles of bronze and iron are **HOLY** to the Lord; they shall go into the treasury of the Lord." (Joshua 6:16-19)*

The seventh chapter of Joshua goes into great detail of the curse that came upon God's chosen people as a result of one man, Achan, who did not keep himself from the tithe which was holy and separated to God.

Tithing is the foundation of God's economic plan. By giving God His first-fruits, he is free to bless us with the blessings of heavenly abundance. I recommend Kenneth Copeland's tape series, "The Laws of Prosperity — The Tithe" as a great teaching on tithing as it relates to the establishing of the covenant between God and His people.

Listen, you can't continue to rob God and be blessed, it doesn't work. It didn't work in Malachi's day, and it doesn't work today either. Give God your best. Be obedient. Let Him prove Himself faithful to His word that

He will pour out of the windows of heaven, a blessing that you don't have room to hold.

TITHING THE TITHE

"Bring the whole tithe into the storehouse, so that there may be food in My house, and test me now in this, says the Lord of hosts, if I will not open for you the windows of heaven and pour out for you a blessing until it overflows." Malachi 3:10

TITHING THE TITHE

Jesus, in rebuking the scribes and Pharisees for their hypocrisy, gave us instruction on how to tithe properly. He said,

> *"You scribes and Pharisees, hypocrites! For you pay tithe of mint and anise and cummin, and have omitted the weightier matters of the law, judgment, mercy, and faith; these ought ye to have done, and not to **leave the other undone"** (Matt. 23:23).*

Of course, tithing was just one of the things that Jesus was referring to, but lets look at this scripture as it relates to tithing. Judgment refers to our righteousness in Christ Jesus. Since we have right-standing with God, we can offer our tithe up as a holy sacrifice to the Lord. Mercy refers to God's love that is within us. Remember the story of the widow's mite. It was her love for God and faith in Him that she gave. It was not important to the Lord how much she gave, as long as she gave from her heart and out of a deep love for her Lord.

Hebrews 11:4 says that

> *"By faith, Abel offered unto God a more excellent sacrifice then Cain, by which (the offering) he obtained witness that he was **RIGHTEOUS,** and God testifying of his gifts."*

Abraham also tithed with faith and righteousness, again before the law of tithing was enacted by Moses. The Bible says,

> *"Melchizedek, king of Salem…was a priest of the Most High, and he (Melchizedek) blessed him (Abram) and said, 'Blessed be Abram of God Most High, possessor of heaven and earth; and blessed be God Most High, who has delivered your enemies into your hand.' And He (Abram) gave him a tenth of all. And the king of Salem said to Abram, 'Give the people to me and take the goods for yourself'. And Abram said to the king of Sodom, 'I have sworn to the God Most High, possessor of heaven and earth, that I will not take a thread or a sandal thong or anything that is yours, lest you should*

say, 'I have made Abram rich.'"
(Genesis 14:18-23)

Abram knew what God had promised. In Genesis 12:2-3, God had promised to bless Abram and make his name great. God is faithful to the promise of His word, for Genesis 13:2 says that Abram was very rich in livestock, and in silver, and in gold. he knew that God would provide, and by using His faith, denied ungodly gains. He staggered not at the promises of God through unbelief (Rom. 4:20).

Notice that Abraham tithed to *the high priest* of the Most High God. This pattern was given to the people of Israel in the law in Deuteronomy 26 through Moses' instruction. I believe that scriptural tithing should follow the pattern set forth in Deuteronomy 26, with New Testament modifications.

"Then it shall be, when you enter the land which the Lord your God gives you as an inheritance, and you possess it and live in it, that you shall take some of the first of all the produce of the ground which you shall bring in from your land that the Lord your God gives you, and you shall put it in a

basket and go to the place where the Lord your God chooses to establish His name.

"And you shall go to the priest who is in office at the time and say to him:, (Note: Tithing is done with the mouth as well as the hand.) "I declare this day to the Lord my God that I have entered the land which the Lord swore to our fathers to give us." Then the priest shall take hold of the basket from your hand and set it down before the altar of the Lord your God.

"And you shall ANSWER and SAY before the Lord your God, "My father was a wandering Aramean, and he went down to Egypt and sojourned there, few in number; but there he became a mighty and populous nation. And the Egyptians treated us harshly and afflicted us, and imposed hard labor on us. Then we cried to the Lord, the God of our fathers, and the Lord heard our voice and saw our affliction and our toil and our oppression; And the Lord brought us out of Egypt with a mighty hand and an outstretched arm and with great terror and with signs and wonders; and He has brought us to this land, a land flowing

with milk and honey, And now behold, I have brought the first of the produce of the ground which Thou, O Lord, hast given me," and you shall set it down before the Lord your God, and worship before the Lord your God; and you shall REJOICE in all the good which the Lord your God has given you and your household.

"When you have finished paying all the tithe of your increase in the third year, the year of tithing, then you shall give it to the Levite, to the stranger, to the orphan and to the widow, that they may eat in your towns, and be satisfied. And you shall SAY before the Lord your God, "I have removed the SACRED PORTION (Remember last chapter!) from my house, and also have given it to the Levite and the alien, the orphan and the widow, according to all Thy commandments which Thou hast commanded me; I have not transgressed or forgotten any of Thy commandments (That's your right-standing before God through the justification by Christ's blood).

"I have not eaten of it while mourning, nor have I removed any of it while I was unclean, nor offered any of it to *the dead. I have listened to the voice of the Lord my God; I have done according to all that Thou hast commanded me. Look down from Thy holy habitation from heaven, and bless Thy people Israel, and the ground which Thou hast given us, a land flowing with milk and honey, as Thou didst swear to our fathers.*

"This day the Lord your God commands you to DO THESE STATUTES and ordinances. You shall therefore be careful to do them with ALL YOUR HEART AND ALL YOUR SOUL. (Deuteronomy 26:1-16)

Most of us have been "plunking something in the bucket" thinking that we were tithing. Actually, the method of tithing was so important that God through Moses and the Holy Spirit wrote an entire chapter about it so that we would KNOW how to tithe. Note that the most important act in tithing is done with the MOUTH, and not the hand. To "tithe" is to confess before the Lord your God through the High Priest of the day, your testimony of what God has done for you personally. Because of your testimony of God's activity in your life, you choose to worship before Him by giving of the very best of what you have.

New Testament tithing is done in very much the same way as in Deuteronomy 26. We make a confession of faith to our High Priest, which is Jesus. Hebrews 3:1 says,

"Consider Jesus, the Apostle and High Priest of our confession."

Have you ever wondered what that confession was? Of course, we confess Jesus as Lord, resulting in our salvation, but it also applies to the confession of our tithe.

At the time of our tithe, we should bring our offering before the Lord, and offer it up to Him through our High Priest Jesus. For me personally, this is done at the time when I write my checks out for the work of God, not when I'm about to "plunk it in the bucket." I go before the Lord and make a confession of my redemption through His blood and confessing my right-standing before God because He has made me the righteousness of God in Christ (2 Cor. 5:20).

I *SAY* these things *out loud* before the Lord, and worship Him with the tithe. Many times He will give me direction at this time to give to the poor, other brothers or sisters in need, or to my local church fellowship. But as I give unto Him, I speak what is in my heart. The Bible says that "Out of the abundance of the heart, the mouth speaks." If your heart is full of the word of God, your tithing confession will be a mighty testimony for God in the earth, and a witness to principalities and powers (Eph. 3:9,10).

I've been asked many times, "Where does the tithe go?" The tithe should go to where the Lord directs you. I believe what Mary, the mother of Jesus said applies here, "Whatever He says unto you, do it." (John 2:15)

There is no New Testament scripture that tells us where to tithe. Many people have been taught that they should tithe to their pastor and give offerings, over and above the tithe, to the rest of the ministry. I do not believe that scripture bears this out. Jesus gave some apostles, some prophets, some evangelists, some pastors and teachers for the equipping of the saints for the work of the ministry (Eph. 4:11,12).

The term "Levites" in the Old Testament was the group representing today's ministers. The tithe generally went to the priests of the day. In the New Testament, the entire church is called "a chosen race, a royal *priesthood,* a holy nation" (I Peter 2:9). We are all priests, if we have been born again by the power of God. Now I'm not saying that pastors shouldn't get the tithe. Stay close with me on this and you'll hear what the Spirit of the Lord is teaching here. In Nehemiah 12:44-47,

> *"All Israel (representative of the Church) gave the portions DUE the singers and the gatekeepers as each day required, and set apart the consecrated portion for the Levite (the priesthood), and the Levites set apart the consecrated portion for the sons of Aaron (the High Priests)."*

Nehemiah 10:39 says,

> *"The sons of Israel and the sons of Levi (the priests) shall bring the contribution of the grain, the new wine*

and the oil, to the chambers; there are the utensils of the sanctuary, the priests who are ministering, the gate-keepers, and the singers."

So scripturally, our tithe and contributions should go to those who are ministering, serving, or singing.

Don't get into bondage with your tithe. If the Lord directs you to send part or all of your tithe to a teacher, or an author, or a TV evangelist, I encourage you to be obedient. Remember that it is the Lord who "supplies seed to the sower" (2 Cor. 9:10), so distribute the seed where He wants and your harvest will be abundantly blessed of God.

7. STEWARDSHIP AND FINANCIAL PLANNING

"For which one of you, when he wants to build a tower, does not first sit down and calculate the cost, to see if he has enough to complete it?" Luke 14:28

STEWARDSHIP AND FINANCIAL PLANNING

There are many Christians today that say we should not budget or plan for our future. They say that we should "not take thought about tomorrow." Let's examine what Jesus said at the Sermon on the Mount.

> *Do not be anxious then, saying, 'What shall we eat?" or 'What shall we drink?' or 'With what shall we clothe ourselves?'. For all these things the Gentiles eagerly seek; for your heavenly Father knows that you need all these things. But seek first His kingdom and His righteousness; and all these things shall be added to you. Therefore do not be anxious for tomorrow; for tomorrow will care for itself. Each day has enough trouble of its own. (Matt. 6:31-34)*

Actually, Jesus was teaching about our attitude toward worry and anxiety, not planning for the future. Jesus tells us not to be anxious about tomorrow. We can certainly plan for tomorrow without being anxious about it. The reason for this is clear: The cares and anxieties of this world are devices that Satan uses to choke the Word of God in your heart so that it becomes unfruitful. (Mark 4:19)

Planning and calculating costs were taught by Jesus in Luke 14:28-32. We must, as Christians, sit down and count the costs in situations we enter. This, I believe, is the biblical foundation for budgeting. By budgeting your income and expenses, you tell your money where to go rather than "wonder where it went."

Certain biblical principles must be adhered to when planning a budget. For example, the tithe of 10 percent of your income must go to the Lord's work. After the tithe to the Lord comes savings. I believe that every person must save at least 10 percent of their net income and possibly even 10 percent of their gross income as an absolute minimum.

This leaves you with 80 percent of your gross income to live on, less taxes and other payroll deductions. You may think that it is impossible to live on only 80 percent but I guarantee to you that it can be done. It may mean doing without that new car with the high payments and insurance and sticking with the 12-year-old jalopy one more year. Maybe you can do without the new living room suite and buy a sofa and chair at a garage sale. You may buy a used lawnmower for $50 instead of charging a new $300 one with all the gadgets that probably won't cut as well. You could even sell your 3 bedroom house and move into a two-bedroom apartment. The pool in the backyard could be substituted with a monthly trip to the beach or to a community park.

You CAN live on 80 percent of your salary. How you sit down and calculate the costs is up to you. It is essential that you set up this system now. The Japanese have succeeded to such a great degree that they now own much of the wealth in American industry and almost 25 percent of the real estate in cities like San Francisco. The major reason that they are a prosperous nation is that each Japanese family saves approximately 18 percent of their gross income before taxes. This tremendous amount of surplus has undoubtedly made them a prosperous nation, both corporately and individually. One month of unemployment would shatter most American's financial house. Following Jesus' principles will assure you of having the resources that you need in any situation. The problem in many American's situations is greed and pride. Neither are godly characteristics. We are to humble ourselves before the Lord and before men. Now, this doesn't mean that you must live like a pauper. On the contrary, you must learn how to be a good steward with what the Lord has given you.

> *He who is faithful in a few things will be put in charge of many things and will enter into the joy of their master (Matt. 25:21).*

That's what I want more than anything else; to enter into the joy of my master, Halleluia!

BARTLING'S FIRST
PRINCIPLE OF FINANCE

If you have to borrow to buy something, you are no more prosperous after you buy it then before you bought it.

In many cases, you are less prosperous. Increasing debt does not increase prosperity. Debt is subtracted from assets to equal net worth. An increase in debt without an increase in assets will ALWAYS decrease net worth.

The next step in budgeting is to determine the differences between needs and wants. If you went to the grocery store and put only necessary items for survival in one cart and everything else in another cart, the difference between wants and needs would be obvious. Seeing them separated makes all the difference in the world.

A budget should not put you in bondage. If it does, you must change it gradually with positive corrective action. A budget is a set of rules that should be adhered to. You are completely free to do whatever you want to within the boundaries you set up yourself. If you "blow it" in one area for the month, you must correct it immediately the next month. But the ideal situation is to work out the budget, then stick to it.

If you have trouble with budgeting and sticking to it, the problem is most likely that you do not like the discipline. You must ask the Lord for help in this area to help you learn to be a "disciple" and discipline yourself in this area.

An excellent and practical book that I recommend to you in money management is Your Money Matters by accountant and financial counselor Malcolm MacGregor. (Bethany House Publishers, Minneapolis, MN).

8. HOW TO GET OUT OF DEBT AND STAY THAT WAY

"Owe no man anything except to love him." Romans 13:8

HOW TO GET OUT
OF DEBT AND
STAY THAT WAY

Each one of you reading this book is in a unique situation in your financial life. You may be able to afford the bills on things that you purchase. My intention is not to dictate to you what things you should buy or not to buy. We know that God has granted to us all things pertaining to life and Godliness through the true knowledge of Him (2 Peter 1:3). He also knows our needs and desires to supply them. Jesus said,

> *Do not be anxious for your life as to what you shall eat, or what you shall drink; nor for your body, as to what you shall put on. Is not life more than food, and the body, more than clothing? Look at the birds of the air, that they do not sow, neither do they reap, neither to they gather into barns, and*

yet your Heavenly Father feeds them. Are you not worth much more than they? And which of you by being anxious can add a single cubit to his life's span? And why are you anxious about clothing? Observe how the lilies of the field grow; they do not toil nor do they spin, yet I say to you that even Solomon in all his glory did not clothe himself as one of these. But if God arrays the grass of the field, which is alive today and tomorrow is thrown into the furnace, will He not much more do so for you, O men of little faith? Do not be anxious then, saying, "What shall we eat?" or "What shall we drink?" or "With what shall we clothe ourselves?." For all these things do the Gentiles seek; for your Heavenly Father knows that you need all these things. But seek first the Kingdom of God and His righteousness and all these things shall be added to you. (Matthew 6:25-33)

This is a familiar passage, yet many truths of God are explained here. First, God is showing us that the things we have come from Him, not from our own work. Our toil does not produce wealth, our faith in God produces wealth. Our reason for working is not to receive "things." Our reason for working to receive wages is to give us the "seed" to plant into God's Kingdom so that our wages NOW go for heavenly treasure. Our earthly blessings from God are measured to us by our measure of planting (Mark 4) either 30-, 60- or 100-fold. Mark 10:30 says we

> *"shall receive a hundred times as much now in the present age, houses and brothers and sisters and children and farms, along with persecutions; and in the age to come, eternal life."*

Many people say that these are spiritual, and I agree, but notice that God has promised a 100-fold return on houses and farms too. When the Body of Christ realizes that God will bless them with a 100 houses or 100 farms, as a measure of their giving, this earth will surely be filled with the glory of God!

God doesn't want a poor people. Solomon in all of his glory did not need food stamps! A lily is not clothed in rags and we shouldn't be either. We must **BELIEVE** that God wants us prosperous and adorned as His church and His bride.

Knowing that God has provided us with our needs, what we must do is align our family economic plan to God's economic plan. God wants His people to be *COMPLETELY FREE FROM THE BONDAGE OF DEBT*.

*"The Lord will command the blessing upon you and your house and in all that you put your hand to ... So all the peoples of the earth shall see that you are called by the name of the Lord ... and you shall lend to many nations, **BUT YOU SHALL NOT BORROW.** And the Lord will make you the head and not the tail (Deut. 28:8-13).*

To live in the blessings of God, a Christian does not have to, and shouldn't borrow.

STEPS TO GETTING OUT OF DEBT NOW

Step 1 — Stop buying on credit immediately!

If you have credit cards, the best method I've found to stop using them is to preheat your oven to 400 degrees, then place your credit cards in the oven on an ungreased cookie sheet and bake for about 5 minutes.

When they have cooled, mail them back to their respective companies.

Excuses that do not work -

EXCUSE 1. *"I need to have receipts for my purchases"*

It is much easier to pay cash and say, "May I have a receipt please?" This is very effective and in all of my experience, I've never been turned down. (You'll be surprised how much time you save at the checkout line by paying cash; the cash line always moves faster!)

EXCUSE 2. *"I pay the cards off every month, so I'm really using "their" money for a month."*

No, you're not. You've paid for the convenience of using the card. You've paid between 3-5 percent of the purchase price for that convenience. If no one used credit cards, the vendor could give everyone a 3-5 percent discount. (Many people who pay cash can ask and receive a cash discount of 3-5 percent) Also, if you have only $20 cash in your pocket, you'll think twice about spending $100 at the store. Making a plan to go to the bank to withdraw the cash or having to write a check, almost always help me to distinguish between a "want" and a "need."

EXCUSE 3. *"I buy only gas on the credit card."*

You will spend several dollars a month on the few cents per gallon you lose by not shopping for the most inexpensive brand of the grade that you like, or paying for the credit card convenience. Your particular station may not be participating in local gas wars that go on all the time.

I know of areas of town that I can save 5-8 cents per gallon just by buying gas when I am in those areas, instead of buying it at the closest station to my house and charging it on the credit card.

EXCUSE 4. *"I don't like carrying a lot of cash."*

You only need to carry a small amount, $10-$20 is plenty to buy gas, food, and miscellaneous expenses for a routine day. You can always carry your checkbook or an ATM (Automatic Teller Machine) card, to let you access your checking account in an emergency.

I've used my ATM card all over the state of Florida and on many business trips. There are also national ATM networks like PLUS that allow you to withdraw cash from any PLUS ATM in the United States.

EXCUSE 5. "I use credit cards when I'm on vacation."

That's the **WORST** time to use your cards, when you're not concerned with everyday expenses! You will always spend more on a vacation if you use credit card versus travelers checks.

When you budget a trip, buy the travelers checks per your budget, plus a little for emergencies, and I guarantee you'll come back from your vacation with a little to spare. A vacation is not restful if you know that you must pay for it when you return.

EXCUSE 6. "I use credit cards for identification."

Almost every place that requires identification for writing checks will accept a check cashing card from a local grocery store as identification. If a business will not take your check, it is your prerogative to stop buying goods from them. Besides, having a credit card in your wallet is no guarantee to the merchant that you don't write bad checks anyway.

Step 2 — Write down a plan for eliminating all of your present debt by paying them off.

List all of your present debts and minimum payments and add up the minimum payments. Commit 15-20 percent of your net income after tithing to reduction of this debt.

If the total of the minimum payments is greater than the 15-20 percent of your net income, you must write the creditors immediately and send them a copy of your written plan.

Example:

Family A has a gross monthly income of $2,000 with the situation below:

Gross Income per Month : $2,000
Less — Taxes, Ins., Payroll Deductions:................ $400
Net Monthly Income: $1,600
Less — Tithe on Gross Income (10%): $200
Net Spendable Income: $1,400

Multiplied times Percentage Committed to Reduce
  Debt... X 20 percent
Monthly Amount to Reduce Debt ....$ 280

Creditors

	Total Balance	Min. Payment
MasterCard	$715...........................	$45
Visa	$400...........................	$30
Sears	$400...........................	$40
J.C. Penney	$300...........................	$25
* Furniture	$1,000..........................	$30
* Car Loan	$3,000........................	$150
TOTAL	$5,815.......................	$320

Estimated Annual Interest 18 percent $1,047
*Secured by collateral

Note that the commitment to debt reduction of $280 per month does not meet the
minimum payment levels set by the creditors. What most families do is pay the $320
or the minimum payments, which leaves the
budget for the month short by $40. Since
they don't have the $40 to pay for genuine
needs, they charge another $100 on credit.
The next month they are in a worse condition as the minimum payments just went up
another $10, leaving them $50 short the next
month. If this situation continues, the interest paid per month will continue to increase,

and the spiral will continue. A family will end up owing more than it could ever repay, just like our national debt situation.

If Family A will stop using credit cards immediately and commit the $280 a month to debt reduction, this plan could be implemented:

Debt Reduction Commitment $280
Less Secured Creditor Payments..............................180
Balance to be paid to Unsecured Creditors $100
(Secured creditors must be paid per your agreement with them, otherwise they will repossess their collateral. In this case, secured creditors are paid their minimum payments, or a total of $180. This leaves a balance of $100 a month to the remaining four creditors.)

	Balance	% of Total Debt
Master Card.........	$ 715............	715/1,815 = 39 percent
Visa...........................	400............	400/1,815 = 22 percent
Sears.........................	400............	400/1,815 = 22 percent
J.C. Penney	300............	300/1,815 = 17 percent

The total debt to these four creditors is $1,815, which at $100 per month, will be paid in full within two years. Using the ratio of each creditor to the total debt, the monthly payments to each are figured:

	percent of Total Debt	Debt Commitment	Actual Payment

MasterCard	.39 X	$100 =	$39
Visa	.22 X	100 =	22
Sears	.22 X	100 =	22
J.C. Penney	17 X	100 =	17

Total Monthly Commitment $ 100

In less than two years, all of the unsecured creditors are paid in full. At that time, the $100 a month can be used to double up on the secured creditors until they are paid in full. In this case, Family A will be completely free of debt in less than three years!

If you use a plan similar to the one above, you **MUST** write to each of the unsecured creditors and tell them of your commitment to pay **ALL** of your indebtedness to them. Commit to them that you will not make any additional charges to the credit line or your credibility for completing the plan will be destroyed. We must, as Christians, keep our word. As long as you make regular payments each month to them per your plan, they will not report any negative comments to the credit agencies. If you do not stick with your plan, they have every right to (and probably will) report you as delinquent or a slow payer.

Step 3 — Eliminate all debt for automobiles.

This is a difficult area for most families because of the desire for all of us to have comfortable, reliable transportation. Most financial analysts recommend spending no more than 20 percent of your net spendable income on transportation expense. This includes loan payments, gasoline, oil, maintenance, insurance and depreciation.

If you are committed to eliminating debt on your automobiles, you must pay off any car debt you have now if you have it. If your credit card debt is paid off, start on doubling up on your car payments.

The sooner you can pay it off, the less interest you'll pay, which is money right down the drain. As soon as your car is paid off, you can start saving the amount you've been spending for car payments! Once its paid off, you may want to self-insure yourself for collision insurance. Depending on where you live, you could save $500 — $1000 a year by having enough cash in savings to replace your car if you did get into an accident. You can increase your deductible on collision insurance as your savings increases.

When you have enough to replace your car if it is totaled, you can discontinue the collision part of your insurance policy. You may have to pay for any collision damage if you do have an accident, but you'll have enough cash in the bank to cover it.

What about buying another car? One good rule of thumb is this — Buy the most reliable, economical, stylish, comfortable car that you can pay cash for. It may not be much, but as the famous bumper sticker says — "Don't Laugh, It's Paid For!."

The best reason for eliminating debt on automobiles is that if the Lord wanted you to give your car away to a brother or sister in need, you can be obedient without having to answer to your debt-master. Proverbs 22:7 says that "the borrower is servant to the lender." We are to be servants of God, not to our local banker.

Step 4 — Avoid borrowing against your home.

Recently, variable rate home equity loans have been very popular. These loans have some good points and some bad points. One of the good points is that the loan interest rate is less than the average for most consumer debt (which is 18.3 percent). The rate is typically several points above the weekly average auction rate of the yield on 6-month Treasury Bills, commonly called T-Bills. Sometimes, banks and savings & loans associations will offer "teaser" rates equal to or slightly higher than the current T-bill rate.

This is usually an attractive rate, usually less than 10 percent a year. The rate then gradually increases on an annual or semi-annual basis to its target rate, usually 3-4 percent above the T-Bill rate. Another good point is that the loans are relatively easy to get, as long as you have equity in your home and are willing to pay the loan application fee (usually several hundred dollars). The disadvantages of these types of loans, however, far outweigh the advantages from a financial planning point of view.

FIRST, they are highly amortized, which means that you pay a very small amount of principal and a very high interest amount with each payment. You could easily end up paying three to four times the original loan amount in interest payments alone.

SECOND, they are secured by the equity in your home.

Many banks advertise these home equity loans as "debt- reconsolidation" loans so that you can pay off your 18 percent debt with a 14 percent home equity loan and lower your monthly payment at the same time.

What they usually don't tell you is that *VISA* or Sears can *NEVER* take your house away from you if you miss a payment, *BUT THE BANK CAN (AND WILL!).* They can start foreclosure proceedings on you to get *THEIR* money out of *YOUR* house.

THIRD, any increase in the value of your home from appreciation or inflation will be siphoned off to the bank as the interest rate changes with inflation rates.

As a last resort, I would considering borrowing against my savings account, credit union share account or taking out a margin loan against my investments at a brokerage firm. If the "borrower is the servant to the lender," than at the very least I am only obligated to serve myself and not others. If you don't have investments or savings to borrow against, you have no business borrowing more from anyone until you do!

I can't stress enough that the secret to getting and staying debt-free is to **MAKE A DECISION TO BE DEBT-FREE,** tithe and ask God to help you every day. If buying on credit is an addiction to you, it must be dealt with as an addiction. God can set you free by the power of the name of Jesus. He does not want you to be bound in the things of this world. I pray that the Body of Christ will continue to mature and give to one another in liberality, as they did in Acts 4:34,35;

> *"For there was not a needy person among them, for all who were owners of land or houses would sell them and bring the proceeds of the sales, and lay them down at the apostles' feet; and they would be distributed to each as any had need." They knew that by giv-*

ing, they put their faith in the provider rather than the provision.

In God's economic system, the way to get improve your standard of living is to give as he directs you to give. A heart that is willing to give to God will be blessed in abundance.

9. INVESTING FOR THE FUTURE

"The wise man saves for the future, but the foolish man spends whatever he gets." Proverbs 21:20

INVESTING FOR THE FUTURE

Most financial planning experts say that you must save a minimum of 10 percent of your net income (after tithing) as a habitual pattern. This savings should be invested in liquid (convertible to cash quickly) accounts. Savings, like tithing, is a discipline and must be made into a habit. If you are not saving 10 percent of your net income now, you can start with 3 or 4 percent. You can work up gradually, like 1-2 percent every couple of months, or whenever you get raises at work. Before you know it, you'll have developed a *habit* of saving.

Savings and investments are not the same thing. Investments are made with dollars over and above the 10 percent savings threshold. You should have at least three months of gross income in savings before considering investments. Investments are not always convertible to cash quickly and should always be separate from savings. Steady plodding should be your method rather than get- rich-quick schemes. The Bible says,

> *"The plans of the diligent lead surely to advantage, but everyone who is hasty comes surely to poverty"* *(Proverbs 21:5).*

Surely, Christians should save **AND** invest. Jesus said,

> *"Then why did you not put the money in the bank, and having come, I would have collected it with interest?"* *(Luke 19:23).*

Saving and investing has been condoned by Jesus. I have heard that God does not want us to have a lot of wealth or investments. They use the "It is harder than a camel to pass through the eye of a needle" scripture. Jesus' disciples answered strangely. They said,

> *"Then how can anyone be saved?"* *(Matthew 19:25).*

Jesus explained that, "with men this is impossible, but with God all things are possible" (Matthew 19:26). God always wants us to believe for the "possible with God" and not strive with the "impossibilities of man"!

Christians should invest "wisely." A wise investment and a conservative investment are not one and the same. One way to invest wisely is to use no-load mutual funds. These funds invest in many different kinds of stocks, bonds and other financial instruments. Buying investments through mutual funds virtually eliminates what is known in finance as "individual investment risk." Because the fund invests in many different instruments, the risk of any particular investment going bad is diversified with the investments that do well. The other type of risk is called "market risk." Market risk is the uncertainty of whether the economy and investment community as a whole will rise or fall.

There is usually only good type of investment during each phase of the normal business cycle. Lately stockbrokers have been pushing "Asset Allocation Funds,"

funds that invest in a mix of cash, stocks and bonds, with the idea that they'll always have protection against catastrophic failure in any particular type of investment. The biggest problem of these types of these asset allocation funds is that, since there is only one good investment at any time in the phase of the business cycle, two-thirds of your investment is always doing poorly.

The wisest investment at any given point can be ascertained by looking at the level and direction of the Prime Interest Rate. Since the Prime changes direction relatively infrequently (maybe once every 12-18 months), determining which investment to be in at specific times in the business cycle does not have to be in a panic. By using a no-load mutual fund family, you can switch from one investment fund to another type of fund with a toll-free telephone call and about 5 minutes.

What about IRA's, retirement plans and company savings plans. The Lord says to "render unto Caesar that which is Caesar's" (Matthew 22:21). We are blessed in this country with many opportunities to shelter our income from "Caesar." I believe with all my heart that God wants us to render unto the Lord's kingdom money that would have gone to Caesar if we didn't have these tax and investment shelters. The more you can save in income tax, the more you'll have left over to do the work of the Lord!

What about life insurance policies as savings, like Universal life or Whole life. *BAD NEWS!* Wise investment counsel would tell you to buy term insurance (the cheapest you can buy) and invest the difference (in your mutual fund family). Also be wary of "Deposit-Term" insurance, a fancy way of charging you for big commissions in year one, so that you can have cheaper rates later. If you'll go through the phone book asking the agents for the cheapest Annual Renewable Term policy that the agent sells, you'll find out how inexpensive it really is.

God want us to be prepared to leave this world today if He comes today, but He also wants us to plan for the future in the event He tarries a little longer.

You can save and invest successfully. Take a course in investments or finance at your local community college or buy a book about investments at your local book store, but be wary of anything with "$1,000,000" in the title.

10. RECEIVING FROM GOD

"But this I say, He which soweth sparingly shall reap also sparingly; and he which soweth bountifully shall reap also bountifully." II Cor. 9:6

RECEIVING FROM GOD

Reaping from God should be easy, but it really isn't. I've heard it said that "God doesn't use the Law of tithing to raise money, He uses it to raise *CHILDREN*"! God created time for man because we needed it. Without God's invention of time, we would never have to learn patience. Ecclesiastes 3:1 says "To every thing there is a season, and a time to every purpose under heaven."

Receiving from God is not "automatic." Haggai 1:5,6 says,

"Now therefore, thus says the Lord of Hosts,'

Consider *YOUR* ways! You have sown much, but harvest little." If we are sowing, but not receiving, we must *CONSIDER OUR WAYS*. The Bible says, "In due season you will reap, IF you faint not" (Galatians

6:9). If you are not reaping, you need a jolt of "faint not"! One thing we can do is "be followers of them who through faith *AND* patience inherit the promises (Hebrews 6:12). The key is "patient endurance." In describing Abraham's receiving, the Bible says that it was *AFTER* he had patiently endured, that he obtained the promise (Hebrews 6:15).

Part of the seed, plant, and harvest principle is watering. We water the seed when we pray in the Spirit (in other tongues). Jesus said.

"Out of your belly shall flow rivers of living water" (John 7:38).

What better fertilizer to the living Word than *LIVING WATER!* "Likewise the Spirit also helps our infirmities; for we know not what we should pray for as we ought, but the Spirit itself makes intercession for us with groanings that cannot be uttered and that He that searches the hearts knows what is the wind of the Spirit, because He makes intercession for the saints according to the will of God. (Romans 8:26,27)

Few believers have experienced the "opened up windows of heaven and blessings that they can't hold in their basket" (Mal 3:11).

I believe the reason for this is three-fold.

FIRST, we haven't planted the seed or we haven't planted in fertile ground. Jesus taught that there is four kinds of ground, but only one kind that produces abundant, lasting fruit. (Mark 4:20)

SECONDLY, we haven't watered the seed through prayer and intercession. We must pray and intercede that the ministries we tithe to and give offerings to will be blessed of the Lord and be prosperous. Most of us complain that we're not getting "our money's worth" when we give to a ministry. We can only be blessed of God in this area if we give unconditionally, just as God gave His Son to us unconditionally. It's only through blessing others that God can bless us. Proverbs 6:2 says that we are "ensnared by the words of our own mouth." We must learn to bless ministries and pray that God will cause them to prosper.

THIRDLY, we have not "cultivated" our crop. Cultivating, or keeping the garden pruned and dressed is the only real job that Adam had before the fall. We have to culti-vate the crop by meditating on the Word of God. The word "meditate" in scripture means to "mutter" or "to roll over and over." I get the picture of a farmer tilling his soil or spading it to keep the weeds out. The Lord wants us to meditate and "roll over" His Word over and over again with an expectant heart. Cultivating by meditating on the Word is a prerequisite for receiving from God (Joshua 1:8).

After we have planted, watered and cul-tivated, it is God's job to cause the growth (I Cor. 3:7). The Bible says we are to "cast our bread upon the waters, and after many days it will be returned to us (Eccl. 11:1). We must believe that God will honor His Word and that our return will be blessed of Him. The psalmist wrote that God has exalted His Word even above His own name, and we know how high that is (Phil. 2:9, Heb. 1:4).

We in America are very blessed as a na-tion and I believe the reason for that is that we are nation founded by godly men for a godly purpose. We were started by a "good seed" in "good ground." We may complain about some of the "branches" of our government, but I believe that the Lord will

> *"prune those branches that do not bear fruit so that the branches that are bearing fruit will bear even more fruit"* (John 15:2).

We, as believers, should not be satisfied with corporate blessings that go to a godly nation. All of our neighbors, whether saved or not saved, enjoy these blessings. Hasn't God got a better plan for us, His chosen children? God wants His Church and its members to be "high on a hill" so that others can see our light. I believe that He wants nations to come from distant lands, bringing their gold and silver with them, to the Church (Is. 60:6) to receive what we have, the very love and wisdom of God. In Solomon's day, the nations came to Him with their wealth because of the godly wisdom that he had been given (I Kings 10:24,25). God wants to do that with us, His Church.

James says,

> *"the testing of your faith produces endurance, and let endurance have its perfect result, that you may be perfect and complete, lacking in nothing. But if any of you lacks wisdom, let Him ask of God, who gives to all men generously and without reproach, and it will be given to him. But let him ask in faith, without any doubting...(James 1:3-6).*

Hebrews 10:36 says,

> *"For you have need of patience that AFTER you have done the will of God, you might receive the promise."*

We receive from God through faith *AND* patience. "Faith comes from hearing and hearing by the Word of God" (Romans 10:17), and the "testing of our faith produces patience" (James 1:3). By studying the Word of God and applying it to our lives, our faith and patience will blossom and we will grow in "receiving from the Lord."

11. HOW TO TRUST GOD FOR BIG THINGS

"If you abide in Me and My words abide in you, ask whatever you wish, and it shall be done for you." John 15:7

HOW TO TRUST GOD
FOR BIG THINGS

In today's day and age, paying cash for a house or a car is the exception rather than the rule. Many people equate home ownership with security. According to the Bible, one has nothing to do with the other. In fact, borrowing to buy a house has the same limitations as borrowing for any other purpose. The Bible does not treat borrowing for a house as okay, and other debt as not okay. Let's face it, it's tough, if not impossible, in today's economy to come up with enough dollars to buy a house. Even if you have the cash to buy one, is it really the wisest use of your resources to pay cash for your home?

My college degree is in Business Finance, bank management and securities analysis, with a minor in accounting. I spent five years in the financial planning and estate planning business so I am not unaware of the world's financial systems. Each one of us, as Christians, have a responsibility to have knowledge of the world's financial systems and influence them by the power of God. Hosea 4:6 says that "My people are destroyed by lack of knowledge." Yet knowledge of the world's financial systems will not bring wealth. In fact, operating in the world's investment market with only carnal (natural) knowledge is very dangerous. Isaiah wrote,

> *"Woe to the rebellious children declares the Lord, who execute a plan, but not Mine, and make an alliance, but not of My Spirit, in order to add sin to sin; Who proceed down to Egypt (the world's system) without consulting Me. To take refuge in the shadow of Egypt!" (Isaiah 30:1-3).*

Many families execute a financial plan on a house without even consulting the Lord. I know that there are Christians who have prayed for a house and the Lord's hand was in the deal and the mortgage. They did go to God first and He did direct them. The Lord blessed them according to their faith. (Matthew 9:29)

If you already have a home mortgage, there are several ways to make pre-payments to your mortgage-holder. You could make b-weekly payments doubling up on the principal portion of each payment or write extra principal-only checks when you get extra funds. Regardless, you really can be debt-free and pay your mortgage off sooner. It doesn't matter right now whether you own a mortgage or home or not; there is only *one* way that you can own a home and be debt-free. That way is *BY FAITH.* Using your faith to pay off your mortgage is a great exercise in faith. And using your faith *PLEASES GOD!* (Hebrews 11:6) When you please the Lord, you can expect the blessings of God to come upon you.

If you are not presently buying a home, and you believe the Lord wants you to have a home, this will be one of the greatest adventures in faith you will ever undertake. The first thing to realize is that trusting God for a paid-for home will take a commitment on your part to step out into a walk of faith.

Many people have never even trusted God for a pair of socks in the morning, much less a house. Your journey will start the moment you **decide** to stand on the Word of the Living God. God said, " I will bless all the work of your hand; and you shall lend to many nations but **YOU SHALL NOT BORROW"** (Deut. 28:12). Our God is a God of Provision, it is His very name "Jehovah Jireh."

Trusting God for a debt-free home will build your faith in other areas. In order to have faith for big things we must be faithful in little things for Jesus said,

> *"He who is faithful in a very little thing is also faithful in much; and he who is unrighteous in a very little thing is unrighteous in much." (Luke 16:10)*

One of the reasons this chapter is near the end of this book is that as you have read God's principles of economics, your faith has been built up by the Word of God. Aligning your personal finances to God's plan for them will build your faith and give you confidence in them. Faith comes by hearing and hearing by the Word of God (Romans 10:17).

As you apply these principles to your family life, you are adding "corresponding action" to your faith. If you really believe that God wants to set you free in finances, you will respond with "corresponding action" for James said

> *"Faith without works (or corresponding actions) is dead, being by itself (James 2:17).*

Just believing that God wants to set you free in finances will not set you free. It will not help you to "try it." We've all heard people moan, "Well, I tried it and it didn't work." They've stated what their problem was all along, they "tried" it instead of "doing" it. See, "doing it" takes faith, "trying it" does not. You can't "try" salvation and see if it works, you have to "do" it. Then you will know that you know that you know it will work, because its working now.

The first step in trusting God for a house is to tithe. This gets you into the "blessing" realm instead of the "cursing" realm. The second step is to get free of all debt, secured and unsecured. The third step is to save according to the plan that God gives you. You'll be surprised at how well it works. When I started saving according to God's plan for a house, it was only about $100 a month. But since God told me to do it, I did it anyway. In 9 months my salary had almost doubled and most of the extra money went into the "house" fund.

As I accumulated enough for a sizeable down-payment, Satan moved in and tempted me to go ahead and buy a house with a mortgage. He brought up this common temptation, " Do you know, Joe, that if you bought a house with the down-payment you have saved, you will be saving over $100 a month from your current rent payment, and you know, that's money right down the drain. And besides, you need the income tax deduction for the interest."

Boy, that sure threw a wrench into God's plan, and everybody I knew agreed with it, even brothers in the Lord. I was impressed of the Lord to spend some time camping in the Florida Keys and to pray about this "new revelation." After several days of fellowship with the Lord, He spoke to me clearer than I had ever heard before. He said, "If you can't trust me for a measly $100 a month, how are you ever going to believe me for a whole house!" Well, I had my answer. No mortgage! When I got back from my trip, my boss called me into his office and gave me a raise of exactly $100 a month! Praise the Lord — He is faithful!

I asked the Lord why more people didn't trust Him for a paid-for house. He said, "They don't ask!" The Bible says, "You have not because you ask not (James 4:2). Many people get exactly what they ask from God. They say, "Lord, help us to get this house while the mortgage rates are only 11 percent and the seller wants to give us a good deal." Well, Jesus said, "You can have what you say." Proverbs 6:2 says, "We are ensnared by the words of our own mouth." It may not have been God's perfect will for you to have that particular house at 11 percent. He may have wanted you to wait until rates were lower, or even another brother in the Lord to give you a house or a place to stay. I got an opportunity to "house-sit" for six months once in a beautiful new furnished home, rent-free! Don't put God in a box. Don't let your desires or lusts for "things" get the better of you. The Bible says that Satan uses certain methods (or schemes) on you. He uses the worries of this world ("Oh we'll never get a house if prices keep going up!"), deceitfulness of riches ("This house will be a good investment and we could make a lot of money on it!"), and the desires for other things ("Everyone else we know is buying a house, why can't we?"). These things enter in and choke the Word of God in your heart so that it becomes unfruitful (Mark 4:19). When Satan is successful in choking the Word in your heart, he will destroy the faith you may have had for the house in the first place. If faith comes by hearing and hearing by the word of God (Romans 10:17), then faith GOES by NOT HEARING the word of God or if it is choked.

From a practical standpoint you can rent a house with a $80,000 mortgage for around $600 a month. That same house would cost you almost $1,000 a month if you had a 30 year mortgage on it at 12 percent. In fact you'd only be paying about $80 in principal and $920 in interest, taxes and insurance with each payment. Living in the same house, you could save the $400 a month difference in a money market fund or CD at 9 percent or 10 percent. If you kept up this savings habit ($400 a month at 10 percent for 10 years), you would have $84,000 in your money market fund or CD. If you had made the $1,000 a month payments, you would have paid only $12,000 towards the principal on your mortgage from your $120,000 worth of payments. Your increase in equity from appreciation (assuming 5 percent inflation) would be only $50,000 (taxable). Your after tax net is over $30,000 greater in only 10 years if you rent rather than buy. This type of mortgage money transfer (your money to the bank) will occur any time that mortgage rates are higher than 9 percent. If you have to borrow at a rate greater than 9 percent, you'd be better off to rent and put the difference into savings and pay taxes on it, rather than paying the higher interest rates. Even from the world's standpoint, it makes no sense at all to borrow at greater than 9 percent. How much less sense should it make to us who know the Biblical consequences of borrowing.

A family home is not to be bought for an investment. A home should be bought only for the security of the family. If the home turns out to be a good investment, that's great! Many home buyers have been lured into buying their home as a "hedge against inflation" or "to build equity." Most new $500 a month mortgage payments allocate about $10 to equity. You could build up equity 10 times faster by saving $100 a month in a savings account.

Brethren, be not deceived by the ways of this world. This ungodly Babylonian system will fall someday, and the only thing left will be that which is firmly planted in the faith of God that put it there. That's why we're taught to "Have the faith of God" (Mark 11:22). It's the only way that the things that we say will come to pass. We will be built on a strong spiritual foundation; the very faith of God Himself, as He has dealt to each of us, the measure of faith.

12. ABUNDANT LIVING THROUGH GIVING

"Give, and it shall be given unto you, pressed down, shaken together, and running over shall men give into your bosom." Luke 6:38

"Freely you received, freely give." Matt. 10:8

ABUNDANT LIVING THROUGH GIVING

God is looking for a giving Church, one that will meet the needs of others. When we rely on the Lord as our source, God can trust us to be obedient to give to those needy people who he brings our way. Needy people are not necessarily the down-and-outers, although they certainly are included. Many ministries "need" satellite time or TV cameras or computers or funds to publish a book that God has called them to write. We must learn not to question the callings of the Lord on others but to be obedient to the leading of the Spirit when it comes to giving.

When the Church gets the revelation of "giving in liberality," then God can "give to us liberally all things." How long will it take us to realize that God's principle of seed time and harvest is the key to our personal prosperity as well as the prosperity of God's Church.

God is in the business of meeting needs. He uses the Body of Christ as His extension on this earth.

> *"For I was hungry, and you gave me something to eat; I was thirsty and you gave me to drink; I was a stranger and you invited me in." (Matt. 25:35)*

Abundant life is the result of giving. Jesus came to give us life and give it more abundantly (John 10:10). Giving is the key to living. Zaccheus picked this up immediately when he met Jesus. He knew that giving to the poor and giving back the money he had defrauded to the people four-fold was the key to living. Jesus said to him,

> *"Today salvation has come to your house, because he, too, is a son of Abraham." (Luke 19:9)*

Jesus was saying that Zaccheus was a man of faith, just like Abraham. He knew that God would be his source, just as Abraham testified in Genesis 14:22,23.

Just as God blessed Abraham, through the high priest, Melchizedek, for his giving, God blesses us through our high priest, Jesus, for our giving. Paul was explaining this principle to the believers at Corinth. In II Corinthians 8, Paul begins to tell the churches at Corinth about what happened to the churches in Macedonia when they started giving. He was specifically referring to the churches at Philippi and Thessalonica. He says,

> *"Now, brethren, we wish to make known to you the grace of God which has been given in the churches of Macedonia, that in great ordeal of affliction their abundance of joy and deep poverty overflowed in the wealth of their liberality. For I testify that according to their ability, and beyond their ability, they gave of their own accord, begging us with much entreating for the favor of participation in the support of the saints, and this, not as we had expected, but they first gave themselves to the Lord and to us by the will of God." (II Cor. 8:1-5)*

Paul was encouraging the Corinthians to give from the heart and not from compulsion. He says,

> *"Your abundance is a supply for their want, that their abundance also may become a supply for your want, that there may be equality" (II Cor. 8:14).*

We see this principle in action in the book of Acts at the peak of the ministry of the apostles.

> *"The congregation of those who believed were of one heart and soul; and not one of them was saying that anything belonging to him was his own; but all things were common property to them. And with great power the apostles were giving WITNESS to the resurrection of the Lord Jesus, and abundant grace was upon them all. For there was not a needy one among them, for all who were owners of land or houses would sell them and bring proceeds from the sales and lay them at the apostles' feet; and they would be distributed to each, as any had need."*
> *(Acts 4:32- 35)*

I believe that a spirit of liberality must come upon today's church for us to be able to move in the resurrection power of the Lord Jesus and to provide an adequate "witness" in the world, just as it did at the hands of the early church. Giving opens the door for God to work mighty miracles as they are manifestations of the abundant grace spoken about in this passage.

As long as today's church is "tight" with their money, which is a manifestation of the spirit of selfishness, they will not know victory. We must come against the powers of selfishness and put them under our feet, once and for all, in the mighty name of Jesus. Once we are free from that evil influence, giving can open the doors to God's miraculous realm.

Without a self-giving, self-denying church as a witness to the world, Jesus cannot come back to earth.

Jesus us told us to "deny ourselves and pick up our cross daily." That includes the sacrifice of giving. But He also knows the "seed" principle, that as we sow into the

Kingdom of God, and are faithful with little, He can trust us to be a greater blessing to the Body of Christ and the needy in our world.

God's promise to those who give sacrificially is clear,

> *"He shall supply all of your needs according to His riches in glory by Christ Jesus" (Phil. 4:19).*

Our heavenly Father is El Shaddei, the God who is "more than enough," but He is also Jehovah Jireh, the Lord of our provision. He is the ram in the thicket, the whale prepared for Jonah, Peter's shadow and the provider of your healing. He is the friend that sticks closer than a brother, and He is the God of *ALL SUFFICIENCY IN ALL THINGS!* Rely on Him as *YOUR PROVIDER*. Give, and it shall be given unto you, pressed down and shaken together and overflowing in your baskets!

ABOUT THE AUTHOR

Joseph Bartling is the President and Founder of Joseph Bartling Ministries and the Shield of Faith Tape Library. Through his prophetic ministry congregations and pastors have been challenged to seek God for the keys to deeper revelation in the Word of God than ever before. His ministry is to bring the message of the five-fold ministry to the Body of Christ and encourage Christians of all denominations to walk in the Spirit.

His free tape ministry reaches into homes all over America to over 5,000 Shield of Faith Tape Library members. They also supply tapes to several missionary outreaches and prison ministries.

The ministry has headquarters in Merritt Island, Florida.

A listing of tapes and books by Joseph Bartling is availableby writing the ministry at:

Joseph Bartling Ministries
P.O. Box 98, Titusville, FL 32781-0098

ABOUT THE SHIELD OF FAITH TAPE LIBRARY

The Shield of Faith Tape Library was started in December, 1984 by Joseph Bartling Ministries as an outreach ministry to the Body of Christ. Today's Church is blessed with an abundance of anointed men and women of God in each of the five-fold ministry given to us byJesus. The offices of pastors, evangelists, teachers, prophets and apostles are all represented in our non-denominational library.

The ministry is free and includes tapes by nearly 200 speakers including Pat Robertson, Kenneth Copeland, Fred Price, Derek Prince, Jamie Buckingham, Benny Hinn, James Robison, David Wilkerson, Malcolm Smith, Arthur Blessitt and Kenneth Hagin.

For the first time in history, each and every believer in God's family can have access to each of the ministries of Jesus through the miracle of multi-media. With an ordinary cassette player, we can "tune our hearts" to the word of God as it is taught, preached and proclaimed by the Church's most popular and anointed servants.

Our tape library is a non-profit ministry which operates solely on the generous free-will offerings and prayers of our library members.You can receive a catalog listing the nearly 3,000 different messages available by sending $3 to cover printing, postage and handling to:

Shield of Faith Tape Library
P.O. Box 98,
Titusville, FL 32781-0098